Playmak

In

The Faith

Vol. 3

Defend The Faith

Scripture References Taken From King James Version / Amplified Bible Classic. Copyright © 1954, 1962, 1964, 1965, 1987 by the Lockman Foundation. All rights reserved.

DEDICATION

Heavenly Father, I pray that this book helps people see the truth in Your Word! I pray that their hearts and minds are open to receive in Jesus name!

CONTENTS

SCRIPTURE

15 But sanctify the Lord God in your hearts: and be **_ready always to give an answer to every man that asketh you a reason of the hope that is in you_** *with meekness and fear:*

1 Peter 3:15 KJV

9 **_He must hold fast to the sure and trustworthy Word of God as he was taught it_**_,_ *so that he may be able both to give stimulating instruction and encouragement in sound (wholesome)* ***doctrine*** ***and to refute and convict those who contradict and oppose it*** *[showing the wayward their error].*

Titus 1:9 AMPC

CHAPTER 1

THE TRUE GOD OF SCIENCE

Thank You, Jesus! Praise Your holy and mighty name! Today, many people rely on science and technology for a variety of things. Science has provided a way for people to better understand God's creation. Many scientists worship a "god of science." They believe the facts and the evidence, but they do not believe in Jesus, who is God. Jesus created the world. Since everything was created by Him, then He is the, **"True God of science."** Science only exists because of God. Without God there is no science. In the book of Genesis, there is a plethora of scientific facts.

The definition of <u>science</u> means: *to know or knowledge*. As followers of Jesus, we know how the world was created and how everything came into existence. Atheists and scientists give theories about how the world came into existence because they **do not know.** Theories are not science. The definition of <u>theory</u>: *a supposition or a system of ideas intended to explain something (Oxford Dictionary of English).* Simply, it means **speculation**. These atheists and scientists do not know how the world came into existence and their theories cannot fit into the category of science. Science is not speculation but facts and truth. We will look at some truths found in the book of Genesis.

Time, Space, and Matter

Time, space, and matter are *unified* and there cannot be one without the other. In the book of Genesis, we see that God created time, space, and matter.

"In the **beginning** God created the **heaven** and the **earth**."
Genesis 1:1 KJV

•**The beginning is** <u>time</u>**. The heaven is** <u>space</u>**. The earth is** <u>matter</u>**.**

In the beginning (TIME),
God created the heavens (SPACE),
and the earth (MATTER).

Sonoluminescence

Sonoluminescence is the scientific phenomena of light coming from sound waves in water. This was first discovered in 1934 and has been performed multiple times in a laboratory. In order for this to happen, they **need water** with a noble gas (*group 18 on periodic table*), and a **sound wave** to **create light**.

"**2** And the earth was without form, and void; and darkness was upon the face of the deep. And the Spirit of God moved upon the face of the **waters**.

3 And **God said** (*sound wave*), Let there be light: **and there was light**."

Genesis 1:2-3 KJV

When God speaks, He creates sound waves. God spoke over the water and light came into existence. Science has proved that this is possible. **This is absolutely not a coincidence**. Moses heard from God about how He created the world. Sonoluminescence is only possible because God created light from His Words in water.

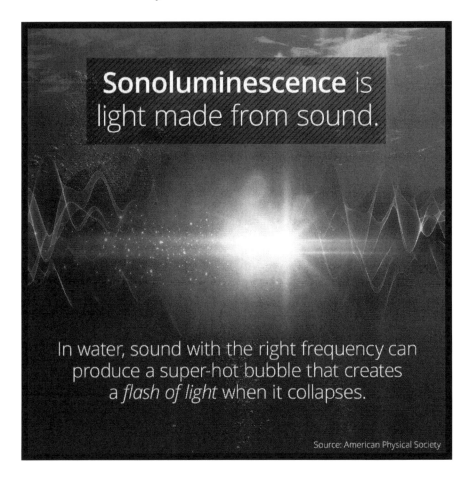

Sonoluminescence is light made from sound.

In water, sound with the right frequency can produce a super-hot bubble that creates a *flash of light* when it collapses.

Source: American Physical Society

Cymatics

Cymatics by definition means *wave*. Science says gravity is the driving force of all matter. Everything in the universe has a frequency including gravity. Frequency is the speed of vibrations and can be measured in Hz. The Law of vibration states that nothing is at rest and all things are moving and vibrating. All vibrations create sound. Some vibrations are very, very low. An atom has a frequency. The frequency is called ELF (Extremely Low Frequency).

"[6] And **God said**, Let there be…"
Genesis 1:6 KJV

"[9] And **God said**…"
Genesis 1:9 KJV

"[11] And **God said**, Let the earth bring forth grass…"
Genesis 1:11 KJV

We can see a pattern here that God spoke (*sound wave*) and things moved, took shape, and form. In the science of cymatics, the sound waves with certain frequencies can cause designs to form in a medium (water, sand).

We see that the Word of God created and shaped the Universe. **The Universe is held together by the Word of God.**

"[3] Who being the brightness of his glory, and the express image of his person, and **upholding all**

things by the word of his power…".
Hebrews 1:3 KJV

     We can say that the sound waves of God are upholding all things.

"In the beginning was the **Word**, and the **Word was with God**, and the **Word was God**.

2 The same was in the beginning with God.

3 **All things were made by him**; and without him was not any thing made that was made."
John 1:1-3 KJV

Immune System & Circumcision

In the Old Testament, under the Mosaic Law, the young males had to be circumcised on the eighth day.

"12 And **he that is eight days old shall be circumcised among you**, every man child in your generations..."
Genesis 17:12 KJV

On the 8th day it has been found by recent studies that the male's immune system is the highest. We know that circumcision is no longer required, but it is amazing to see why God was so specific on choosing the 8th day.

Here is a quote from: **Biblical Accuracy and Circumcision on the 8th Day**

By, Bert Thompson Ph.D.

On the eighth day, the amount of prothrombin present actually is elevated **above one-hundred percent of normal** —and is the only day in the male's life in which this will be the case under normal conditions. If surgery is to be performed, day eight is the perfect day to do it. Vitamin K and prothrombin levels are at their peak. The chart below, patterned after one published by S.I. McMillen, M.D., in his book, *None of These Diseases*, portrays this in graphic form.

Dr. McMillen observed:

We should commend the many hundreds of workers who labored at great expense over a number of years to discover that the safest day to perform circumcision is the eighth. Yet, as we congratulate medical science for this recent finding, we can almost hear the leaves of the Bible rustling. They would like to remind us that four thousand years ago, when God **initiated** circumcision with Abraham....

Abraham did not pick the eighth day after many centuries of trial-and-error experiments. Neither he nor any of his company from the ancient city of Ur in the Chaldees ever had been circumcised. It was a day picked by the Creator of vitamin K (1984, p. 93).

Moses' information, as recorded in Genesis 17:12, not only was scientifically accurate, but was years ahead of its time.

REFERENCES

Holt, L.E. and R. McIntosh (1953), *Holt Pediatrics* (New York: Appleton-Century-Crofts), twelfth edition.

McMillen, S.I. (1984), *None of These Diseases* (Old Tappan, NJ: Revell).

CHAPTER 2

SUBSTANTIAL EVIDENCE

Praise the Lord for He is good! Thank You, Lord, for giving us your Word which is truth. We worship You because You are the Creator of the heavens and the earth. Your great and magnificent works are seen throughout creation.

Substantial evidence by definition: *an individual piece of evidence that is sufficient, so that a person with a sound and reasonable mind could convict or acquit on that piece of evidence.*

There is substantial evidence that the Bible is supernatural and true. The Bible has over 40 different authors. It has been written over a time period of 1,600 years. These authors in the Bible wrote on three different continents in three different languages. Their words are all in agreement with one another. Many of them prophesied about future events that came true. This is supernatural.

Simon Greenleaf, a professor and Doctor of Law, wrote a book called, **Testimony of the Evangelists**. He was an atheist at one point in his life. His students challenged him to put the Christian faith on trial. He used the substantial evidence rule. This professor, who helped start the Harvard School of Law, has stated that the resurrection of Jesus Christ is true. There was over 500 witnesses and many of those witnesses are credible sources.

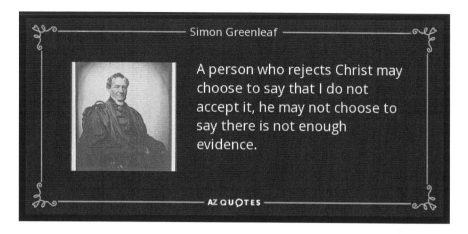

Simon Greenleaf

A person who rejects Christ may choose to say that I do not accept it, he may not choose to say there is not enough evidence.

AZ QUOTES

Another book that has credible evidence is written by Josh McDowell. ***The New Evidence That Demands a Verdict***. He was also once an atheist who tried to prove that Christianity was false and later became a Christian because of the overwhelming evidence.

One thing that atheists cannot do is prove that God does not exist. They always try to have Christians prove that He does exist, but they can never prove that He doesn't exist. There is no substantial evidence for any of their statements. All of their statements are based on assumptions.

CHAPTER 3

GOD IS OMNIPOTENT

Praise the Lord for His mercy and grace! The God that we serve is Omnipotent- **all powerful**. The Bible tells us this in Revelation 19:6.

> ⇒"**6** And I heard as it were the voice of a great multitude, and as the voice of many waters, and as the voice of mighty thunderings, saying, Alleluia: for the **Lord God omnipotent** reigneth."
> **Revelation 19:6 KJV**

There are some theologians who teach that God is omnipresent- *present everywhere at all times* and omniscient- *all knowing*. Let's look at some Scripture to see if these statements are true about the God we serve.

Some Christians have stated that God is present everywhere at all times- *omnipresent*.

The **definition of presence** - *being at hand, the state or fact of existing, occurring or being present*. (*Oxford Dictionary of English*)

The **definition of everywhere** – *in or to all places, all places or directions. (Oxford Dictionary of English)*

- This would mean that the Holy Spirit fills **100%** of the earth, atmosphere, outside & inside buildings, water, and everything that exists.

Let's look at the Scriptures people use to back up these statements.

23 *"Am I a God at hand, saith the Lord, and not a God afar off?*

24 *Can any hide himself in secret places that I shall not **see** him? saith the Lord. **Do not I fill heaven and earth**? saith the Lord."*
Jeremiah 23:23-24 KJV

- What does the Lord fill heaven and earth with? Does He fill it with His **presence** or **creation**? In Genesis, chapter 1:1, God created the heaven and the earth. In verse 2, it says the earth was without form and void (*empty*).

Hebrew word **bohuw**: *emptiness, void, waste.*

God created water, land, creatures, and humans <u>to fill it</u>.

20 And God said, **Let the waters bring forth abundantly the moving creature** that hath life, and fowl that may fly above the earth in the open firmament of heaven.

22 And God blessed them, saying, **Be fruitful, and multiply, <u>and fill the waters</u> in the seas**, and let fowl multiply in the earth.
Genesis 1:20,22 KJV

Here is another Scripture that is used to prove that God is present everywhere at all times.

7 Whither <u>**shall I go from thy spirit**</u>? <u>**or whither shall I flee from thy presence**</u>?

8 If I ascend up into heaven, thou art there: **if I make my bed in hell, behold, <u>thou art there</u>.**

9 If I take the wings of the morning, and **dwell in the uttermost parts of the sea;**

¹⁰ Even there shall thy hand lead me, and thy right hand shall hold me.
Psalm 139:7-10 KJV

This is a psalm by King David of Israel. King David was also a prophet (*Acts 2:29-30*). Prophets in the Old Testament had the Spirit of God because they could only prophesy by His Spirit. Not everyone who believed in God had the Holy Spirit. There were only few who had the Holy Spirit dwell with them (*Numbers 27:18, Judges 3:10, 1 Samuel 10:10*). This verse does not and cannot imply that the Holy Spirit is with everyone and everywhere at all times. The Holy Spirit was with David. Wherever David went the Holy Spirit was with him. Context is very important!

Here is another Scripture.

³ The eyes of the Lord <u>are in every place</u>, beholding the evil and the good.
Proverbs 15:3 KJV

Many assume that because God has eyes everywhere that His presence must be there. Why do we fail to think that God can be on His throne in

Heaven and see everything? Men have the capability to see football games in other states and countries without physically being there. This is done through television. Why do we limit God and say that His presence must be there in order for Him to see what is going on? There are cameras in many places which allow government officials to see without their presence being there.

⇒<u>God is Supernatural and all powerful</u> (**omnipotent**). He can record everything and *choose* what He wants to see at any time. It also doesn't mean that He is watching everything <u>at all times</u>. He gave angels tasks and work to do. They send messages and help watch over His people. There will be books that will be opened up on Judgement Day that keep record about our lives (*Revelation 20:12-15*).

To say that the Holy Spirit is present everywhere at all times would be a direct contradiction to these Scriptures.

5 And **the Lord came down to see** the city and the tower, which the children of men builded.
Genesis 11:5 KJV

9 After this manner therefore pray ye: **Our Father which art in heaven**, Hallowed be thy name.
Matthew 6:9 KJV

2 The **Lord looked down from heaven** upon the children of men, to see if there were any that did understand, and seek God.
Psalm 14:2 KJV

24 God that made the world and all things therein, seeing that he is Lord of heaven and earth, **dwelleth not in temples** made with hands;
Acts 17:24 KJV

8 And they heard the voice of the Lord God walking in the garden in the cool of the day: and Adam and his wife **hid themselves from the presence of the Lord God** amongst the trees of the garden.
Genesis 3:8 KJV

16 And Cain **went out from the presence of the Lord**, and dwelt in the land of Nod, on the east

of Eden.
Genesis 4:16 KJV

7 So went Satan forth **from the <u>presence</u> of the Lord**, and smote Job with sore boils from the sole of his foot unto his crown.
Job 2:7 KJV

10 Create in me a clean heart, O God; and renew a right spirit within me.

11 Cast me not away from thy <u>presence</u>; and <u>take not thy holy spirit from me</u>.
Psalm 51:10-11 KJV

14 If my people, which are called by my name, shall humble themselves, and pray, and seek my face, and turn from their wicked ways; **then will I hear from heaven**, and will forgive their sin, and will heal their land.
2 Chronicles 7:14 KJV

> ⦾ If the Holy Spirit is present everywhere, why do we pray and worship to invite His presence with us? If He was already present, we wouldn't need to

ask or invite Him with us. **The Holy Spirit can be multiple places at once, because we as believers who obey God, have His Holy Spirit living inside of us (***Acts 5:32, John 14:17, John 14:21-26***)**. But, to say His Holy Spirit is **everywhere** at once **at all times** is completely unscriptural.

- Is the Holy Spirit present at all times in a satanic temple, full of satanists conjuring up demonic spirits?

- I asked this question to some people who believed in the Holy Spirit being omnipresent. They answered and said yes. That is sad and disturbing that Christians would say the Holy Spirit dwells in a satanic temple.

- ***Dwell definition-*** *tarry, remain in a place.*

- ***Omnipresence of God comes from New Age religion and it is demonic***!

20

⇒**2 Corinthians 6:14-18, Isaiah 59:2** (*sin causes separation from God*).

- **Separation definition**- *the action or state of moving or being moved apart.*
- If the Holy Spirit is present everywhere at all times how can anyone be separated from God?

- **I believe that God is omnipresent in Heaven.** His Holy Spirit is everywhere in Heaven because everyone and everything is Holy. No evil shall dwell with the Lord. (*Psalm 5:4*)

Is God Omniscient?

⇒ If God knew before He created the devil, that the devil would rebel against Him, and <u>without a doubt</u> choose evil, why did He create him?

⇒ Would God **<u>knowingly</u>** create a being just for it to suffer in extreme torment forever? Is this part of His big plan to **knowingly** create beings and eventually destroy it?

These questions are not good, and they can make God seem evil.

My question is, **"Did God know that the devil was going to rebel against Him?"** There is no clear answer in the Bible.

I truly believe that God **did not know** the devil was going to rebel against Him and I believe that God was grieved (*hurt emotionally*) when the devil rebelled.

God created the devil and **He created him good (***Ezekiel 28:12-15***)**. God **loves all of His creation**. God gave the devil free will to choose. Choice and free will allows for there to be a genuine real fellowship. **God desires love and fellowship over knowledge (*or to know everything*).** If you knew everything your spouse was going to think, say, or do, would it be interesting or a desirable relationship?

The opportunity existed for the devil to resist and rebel against God, but I believe **God hoped that none of His creation would choose evil** (*Isaiah 14:12-15*). God desires that **ALL** men be saved, and that none perish. Not all men and women will choose to have a relationship with God. (*1 Timothy 2:4. Ezekiel 33:11*)

⇒<u>**I believe that God chooses to not know certain things.**</u>

⇒**God is certainly <u>powerful enough</u> to know everything if He wanted to**.

- I believe He chooses to not know certain things for the sake of **love, fellowship, trust, and creation's free will.**

- *For God to **not** know certain things doesn't make Him less powerful. He just desires **a real (sincere)** relationship with His creation, **more than knowing everything**. If God* *knew beforehand which ones of His creation would rebel against Him, I believe He wouldn't have created them. I believe He hid that knowledge from Himself in order to create us and give us free will to choose Him or not.*

*God's Son **chose** to humble Himself and come to the earth in the flesh, and die for the sins of His creation. Man exalts knowledge, but God exalts mercy and love!*

4 Look not every man on his own things, but every man also on the things of others.
5 Let this mind be in you, which was also in Christ Jesus:

6 **Who, being in the form of God, thought it not robbery to be equal with God:**

7 But made himself of no reputation, and ***took upon him the form of a servant, and was made in the likeness of men:***

8 And **being found in fashion as a man, <u>he humbled himself</u>, and became obedient unto death, even the death of the cross.**
Philippians 2:4-8 KJV

⇒ **¹⁹** And **to know the love of Christ, which passeth knowledge**, that ye might be filled with all the fulness of God.
Ephesians 3:19 KJV

Think about this. God's Son humbled Himself when He walked amongst men and He has the same mindset as His Father. The Greek definition for **humbled** – *to make low, bring low, to assign to a lower rank, to be ranked below others, to have a modest opinion of one's self, devoid of all haugtiness.*

　　　 ○**His love for us surpasses all knowledge.**

　　Let's look at some Scripture that would back up my statement that God has <u>chosen</u> to limit His knowledge.

And out of the ground the Lord God formed every beast of the field, and every fowl of the air; and **brought them unto Adam to see what he would call them**: and whatsoever Adam called every living creature, that was the name thereof.

Genesis 2:19 KJV

God brought the animals to Adam <u>to see</u> what he would call them.

26 And he said, **So is the kingdom of God**, as if a man should cast seed into the ground;

27 And should sleep, and rise night and day, and the seed should spring and grow up, **he knoweth not how**.

28 For the **earth bringeth forth fruit of herself**; first the blade, then the ear, after that the full corn in the ear.

29 But when the fruit is brought forth, immediately **he putteth in the sickle**, because the harvest is come.

Mark 4:26-29 KJV

God has created the earth to operate on its own. He has given laws for the heavens and earth. God has given man free will to choose and the ability to make his or her own decisions.

In the book of Revelation, we can see the One who has the sickle and reaps the harvest of the world from Mark 4.

¹⁴ And I looked, and behold a white cloud, and upon the cloud one sat like unto the **Son of man, having on his head a golden crown, and in his hand a sharp sickle.**

¹⁵ And another angel came out of the temple, crying with a loud voice to him that sat on the cloud, Thrust in thy sickle, and reap: for the time is come for thee to reap; **for the harvest of the earth is ripe**.
Revelation 14:14-15 KJV

God is Sovereign.

Definition of sovereign: *a supreme ruler, possessing supreme power*.

Notice it doesn't say ALL CONTROLLING.
Sovereign does not mean that God controls everything. God does not control our thoughts and man does have his own will (*Matthew 15:19, John 1:13*).

1. **God is not in complete control of who chooses Him**. God has revealed Himself so that anyone can seek after Him. **Anyone**

who has a heart of **repentance and humility** to seek after God will find Him.

2. God has put the responsibility in our hands. Adam was commanded to work and take care of the earth. We have to pray for others and ask God to intervene to combat the evil in this world. The Lord gave us dominion and authority over the animals and the earth. (*Genesis 1:26-30*)

26 And hath made of one blood all nations of men for to dwell on all the face of the earth, and hath determined the times before appointed, and the bounds of their habitation;

27 **That they should seek the Lord**, if haply they might feel after him, and find him, though he be not far from every one of us:
Acts 17:26-27 KJV

There are times when God will choose certain people to carry out His will/plan before they are born. Example: Moses, Jeremiah, and the 12 Disciples.

God knows men by searching their hearts and their thoughts. God can influence a man's thoughts or actions, but that man has to be <u>willing</u>. Similar to a dad influencing his sons actions or thoughts with his words and actions. God does have plans for our lives, but we have to be **willing** to walk in His perfect plan.

"And thou, Solomon my son, know thou the God of thy father, and serve him with a perfect **heart** and **with a willing mind**: for the Lord **searcheth all hearts**, and understandeth all the imaginations of the thoughts: **<u>if thou seek him, he will be found of thee</u>**; but if thou forsake him, he will cast thee off for ever."
1 Chronicles 28:9 KJV

6 Now there was a day when the sons of God came to present themselves before the Lord, and Satan came also among them.

7 And the **Lord said unto Satan, Whence comest thou**? Then Satan answered the Lord, and said, From going to and fro in the earth, and from

walking up and down in it.
Job 1:6-7 KJV

If God already knew where the devil was beforehand and He knew that he was about to come into His presence, why ask him where did you come from?

⁶ And it repented the Lord that he had made man on the earth, and it grieved him at his heart.

⁷ And the Lord said, <u>I will destroy man whom I have created from the face of the earth</u>; both man, and beast, and the creeping thing, and the fowls of the air; **for it <u>repenteth me that I have made them</u>**.
Genesis 6:6-7 KJV

Did the Lord know beforehand that He would regret creating man and later destroy man? Why would God **knowingly** create something that He would later end up destroying?

20 And **the Lord said**, Because the cry of Sodom and Gomorrah is great, and **because their sin is very grievous**;

21 I will go down now, and see whether they have done altogether <u>according to the cry of it</u>, which is come unto me; and **if not, I will know**.
Genesis 18:20-21 KJV

Did the Lord know beforehand about everything that was going on in Sodom and Gomorrah? If we say that He already knew before it happened, then we would be calling God a liar. If God knew, then He would be lying to Abraham. God is not a man that He should lie. God is telling Abraham, "_If not, I will know_." God is telling Abraham that He did not know. God heard the cry of their sin but He went to see if it was true before He would destroy it.

30 **And Jephthah vowed a vow unto the Lord, and said, If** thou shalt without fail deliver the children of Ammon into mine hands,

31 Then it shall be, that whatsoever cometh forth of the doors of my house to meet me, when I return in peace from the children of Ammon, shall surely be the Lord's, and **I will offer it up for a burnt offering**.

32 So Jephthah passed over unto the children of Ammon to fight against them; **and the Lord delivered them into his hands.**
Judges 11:30-32 KJV

34 And Jephthah came to Mizpeh unto his house, and, behold, **his daughter came out to meet him with timbrels** and with dances: and she was his only child; beside her he had neither son nor daughter.

35 And it came to pass, when he saw her, that he rent his clothes, and said, Alas, my daughter! thou hast brought me very low, and thou art one of them that trouble me: for **I have opened my mouth unto the Lord, and I cannot go back.**
Judges 11:34-35 KJV

If the Lord knew beforehand that Jephthah's daughter was going to come out of the house first to meet him, why did the Lord God grant him victory? Isn't God against human sacrifice? This is the only human sacrifice in the bible.

For I will be merciful to their unrighteousness, and their **sins** and their iniquities will I **remember no more**.
Hebrews 8:12 KJV

God <u>chooses</u> to not remember sins. Let's not say, "He has to be Omniscient or He can't be God." The bible doesn't fully support that statement without contradicting itself.

When I tell atheists that I believe God chose to limit His knowledge, they listen. It surprises them because they have not heard many people talk about God <u>choosing</u> to limit His knowledge. They usually have nothing else to refute because the contradictions that they believed about God have been removed.

- There are also some modern Christian theologians who also believe that God chooses to limit His knowledge.

CHAPTER 4

RELIGIOUS BELIEFS & DIFFERENCES

Praise God! There are many beliefs and religious views in the world today. Many people have become confused because of the variety of beliefs. They believe that there are many ways to get to God. In Christianity, we believe that Jesus is the only way to God. No one comes to God except through Jesus alone (*John 14:6*). This is the TRUTH!

Christianity says that 1+1=2. The other religions say that 1+1=3. We know for a fact that 1+1 does not equal 3. Many people want us to believe that it equals 3, and so does the devil.

I personally could not tolerate someone going around saying that 1+1=3. I would lovingly correct them and teach them the truth. In order to have confidence in the faith, we have to study and meditate on the Word daily.

We Do Not Serve The Same God

People claim that Christians, Muslims, and Jews all serve the same God. This lie is taught in schools and Universities. The truth is that we do not serve the same God. Islam and Judaism do not teach that Jesus is Christ the Messiah.

22 **Who is a liar but he that denieth that Jesus is the Christ**? He is antichrist, that denieth the Father and the Son.
23 **Whosoever denieth the Son, the same hath not the Father**: he that acknowledgeth the Son hath the Father also.
1 John 2:22-23 KJV

⊙**Whoever does not believe in Jesus as their Lord and Savior, does not know and worship our God!**

Racism & Slavery

There is a group of people who call themselves the Black Hebrew Israelites. Their whole belief is based on the color of their skin and pride. This group that is rising up is similar to Adolf Hitler in pride in their race. Adolf Hitler lifted up the Aryan race. The Black Hebrew Israelites are similar in thought by lifting up their race, but not the same in deeds. They are not killing innocent people. In reality, we should be lifting up each other and anyone who wants to receive Jesus.

Many of these groups use foul language and hate speech but call themselves people who worship God. (*James 1:26*)

There is another group who believes in Kemetic Science and African Ancestors. They claim

that Christianity is the white man's religion. They also say that the Bible is used to promote a form of slavery.

If I'm not mistaken, the ancient Egyptians who were people of brown skin, enslaved the tribes of Israel for over 400 years. Many of those tribes were brown skinned people as well. This was **not** white or Caucasian people enslaving black people.

It was brown people enslaving a group of people who were of different nationalities. <u>This is a horrible **excuse** as to why they try to refute the Bible</u>.

Just because people of your own skin color practiced a certain religion or belief, does not make it the truth. All of those other religions believe in many gods and witchcraft. I believe in One God. I believe in Jesus as Lord. I am a Christian. A Christian, by definition, is a follower of Jesus Christ. I follow the commands of Jesus (*1 John 2:3-5*). The Bible is the truth and everything else is a lie. **Jesus is the ONLY WAY, THE TRUTH, AND THE LIFE!**

CHAPTER 5

JESUS IS LORD

Thank You, Jesus! I spend a lot of my time ministering to people of all races and beliefs. I have ministered to many atheists and scientists who do not believe in God. I have even ministered to Christians who left the faith and have become atheists or Satanists.

I remember ministering to an atheist who once was a Christian and his three friends. He asked me to give him evidence that God exists. I gave him scientific facts in the Bible. His friends who were Christians were in shock at the evidence that I gave him. The young man told me that it was just a coincidence. Once I see that certain people are hard hearted and still refuse to believe even after they were given evidence, I then give them the hardcore truth.

I did not have a choice over my birthday, September 29th, 1986. I had no choice over my height, skin color, talents, or who my parents would be. When I came into this world, my opinion or belief did not change what was truth. I do have a choice whether I want to serve God or not. My personal belief adjusted to the **TRUTH**.

There is a real Heaven and Hell. It doesn't matter what anyone on this earth believes. Nobody can change that fact. Nobody can change the fact that we will all die one day. It is inevitable that everyone will face death. Nobody can run from the Judgement Seat of Christ. Therefore, if people do not repent and accept Jesus as their Lord and Savior, they will die in their sins and burn in Hell forever.

Many do not want to change their life. They like the sinful pleasures of this world. **Remember,** sin is only for a short season and then comes eternal suffering. Is temporary pleasure worth eternal suffering?

25 **Choosing rather to suffer affliction with the people of God, than to enjoy the <u>pleasures of sin for a season</u>;**
26 Esteeming the <u>reproach of Christ greater riches</u> than the treasures in Egypt: for he had respect unto the recompence of the reward.
Hebrews 12:25-26 KJV

Whoever does not want Jesus to be their Lord, will suffer the consequences. I pray they repent and turn to faith in Jesus.

14 **But his citizens hated him**, and sent a message after him, saying, **We will not have this man to reign over us. 27 But those mine enemies, which would not that I should reign over them, bring hither, and slay them before me.**
Luke 19:14,27 KJV

Evil & Death

A lot of people fault God for allowing the evil in this world. They blame God for cancer, sickness, and tragic deaths to their family members. Many don't realize that the devil has authority in this world. When Adam sinned against God, his authority was handed over to the devil (*Luke 4:6*). The devil has the power of death over non-believers (*Hebrews 2:14*). Everyone that is born into this world is born under the kingdom of darkness (*1 John 5:18-19*). Jesus says that the **devil comes to steal, kill, and destroy** (*John 10:10*). The devil can bring sickness upon people and keep them in bondage for years (*Luke 13:11-16*). **God is not the one at fault**. Evil is the devil's doing and people are submitting to his influence. Sin opens the door for the enemy (*Ephesians 4:27*). The devil is the master of deception; after all, he deceived 1/3 of the angels in Heaven. (*Revelation 12:4-9*)

When people die, if they did not believe in Jesus and did not live a life pleasing to the Lord, they are **not** resting in peace.

Death should not only be seen as something bad. Death is good for those who believe in Jesus (*Philippians 1:21*). When followers of Jesus die, they enter into Heaven where there is eternal peace, love, joy, and happiness. This is a very good thing. Followers of Jesus should be looking forward to death. In this world, there is pain, suffering, and torment. The reason God said Adam would die, is so that sin and death would not exist forever. If we lived forever in this world, there would be constant suffering. Death brings an end to the pain and suffering for followers of Jesus. The ones who reject Jesus, will experience pain and suffering forever.

Prayers aren't answered

Let's look at some Scripture to see why some prayers aren't answered.

³¹ We know that God does not listen to sinners; but if anyone is God-fearing *and* a worshiper of Him and **does His will**, **He listens to him.**
John 9:31 AMPC

21 The person who has My commands and keeps them is the one who [really] loves Me; and whoever [really] loves Me will be loved by My Father, and I [too] **will love him and will show (reveal, manifest) Myself to him**. [I will let Myself be clearly seen by him and make Myself real to him.]
John 14:21 AMPC

5 If any of you lack wisdom, **let him ask of God, that giveth to all men liberally**, and upbraideth not; and it shall be given him.
6 **But let him ask in faith, nothing wavering**. For he that wavereth is like a wave of the sea driven with the wind and tossed.
7 **For let not that man think that he shall receive any thing of the Lord.**
8 A double minded man is unstable in all his ways.
James 1:5-8 KJV

2 **You are jealous and covet [what others have] and your desires go unfulfilled;** [so] you become murderers. [To hate is to murder as far as your hearts are concerned.] You burn with envy and anger and are not able to obtain [the gratification, the contentment, and the happiness that you seek], so you fight and war. You do not have, because you do not ask.

3 [Or] **you do ask [God for them] and yet fail to receive, because you ask with wrong purpose and evil, selfish motives. Your intention is [when you get what you desire] to spend it in sensual pleasures**.
James 4:2-3 AMPC

1. **If someone's prayers are not being answered they need to ask themselves, "Am I living a life of sin?"**

   2. **"Am I obeying the commandments of Jesus?"**

   3. **"Am I praying for God's will or my will?"**

   4. **"Did I truly believe that God would answer my prayer?"**

⇒We also must remember that sometimes God answers prayers, just not in the way we thought He would.

We are renting the earth. The Lord owns it, but He has allowed us to live in it and take care of it. God, who is the Landlord, has given us rules to obey. If we keep those rules, He will hear our prayer for help. If we do not keep those rules and disrespect them, He will not listen. His rules are good. If we choose to not obey them, then we are choosing to be evil.

One day, the lease will be up. Depending upon how we live will determine if we are upgraded to live with Him in Heaven or cast away to Hell. It's our choice. Choose wisely and choose **LIFE**!

- **Pray for those who have a hard heart towards God.**
- **Be patient with those who are lost when ministering to them.**
- **Use this knowledge in love, to help lead others to Jesus.**

Printed in Great Britain
by Amazon